ALASKA BROWN BEAR

GIANTS AMONG US

Jason Cooper

Rourke Book Co., Inc.
Vero Beach, Florida 32964

Edited by Pamela J.P. Schroeder

PHOTO CREDITS
All photos © Lynn M. Stone

Library of Congress Cataloging-in-Publication Data
Cooper, Jason, 1942-
    Alaska brown bear / by Jason Cooper.
        p.   cm. — (Giants among us)
    Includes index.
    Summary: Describes the physical characteristics and habits of
the large bears that thrive on the southern coast of Alaska.
    ISBN 1-55916-183-3
    1. Kodiak bear—Juvenile literature. 2. Brown bear—Alaska—
Juvenile literature.   [1. Kodiak bear. 2. Brown bear. 3. Bears.]
I. Title. II. Series: Cooper, Jason, 1942-   Giants among us.
QL737.C27C665   1997
599.784—dc21   95-52097
                                                       CIP
                                                        AC

Printed in the USA

TABLE OF CONTENTS

ALASKA BROWN BEAR

Brown bears can't shop for new homes. If they could, they might all choose the seacoasts of southern Alaska.

Brown bears are about the same wherever they live—North America, Europe, or Asia. The brown bears of Alaska's coasts, however, are the biggest and most plentiful brown bears anywhere.

It seems that the big bears of southern Alaska eat better than their cousins. These coastal brown bears fatten up on **salmon** (SAH mun) each summer.

Just a mile from the sea, a crowd of brown bears fishes for salmon along the falls of Alaska's McNeil River.

GIANTS OF THE COASTS

Alaska's biggest coastal brown bears are the largest land **carnivores** (KAR nih vorz), or meat-eaters, on Earth. Big males can top 1,700 pounds (773 kilograms) and 5 feet (1.5 meters) tall at the shoulder.

When a big brownie stands on its hind feet, it's *really* big! It can be 10 feet (3 m) tall—the height of a basketball rim.

Brown bears don't walk on their hind feet. They sometimes stand, though, for a better look at their surroundings.

Standing on their hind feet, Alaska brown bears may be 10 feet (3 m) tall.

WHERE BROWN BEARS LIVE

Alaska's coastal brown bears live along the state's southern coasts and nearby islands. The largest bears are on Kodiak Island.

Brownies prowl beaches, mud flats, meadows, river valleys, and brushy hillsides.

Brown bears in other parts of Alaska and North America are called grizzlies. Grizzlies are smaller than coastal brown bears. Grizzlies usually have more silver-tipped fur than brownies.

The mud flats, hillsides, and meadows of southern Alaska are homes for brown bears.

CUBS, THE BABY BEARS

Brown bears are born while their mother sleeps in her snug winter den. The mother usually has two cubs.

At birth, cubs are little giants. They weigh no more than 1 1/2 pounds (680 grams).

By springtime the cubs are plump and playful. The mother bear leads them from the den. For the next three or four years, the cubs will stay with their mother.

If it's quick enough, this two-year-old cub will share a salmon meal with its mother. Cubs have to take food.

11

Big, broad-headed brown bears of Kodiak Island are the largest of the world's land carnivores.

*An Alaska brown bear splashes ashore on a mid-summer day
with its prize, a chum salmon.*

BROWN BEAR FOOD

Even though they are the largest carnivores on Earth, Alaska's brown bears don't always eat meat. Like cattle, brown bears walk through meadows and **graze** (GRAYZ) on green plants.

Some brownies have a taste for razor clams. They dig up the clams on Alaskan beaches.

Salmon are the bears' main food in summer. In fall they feed on ripe berries. Sometimes brown bears eat dead animals.

A brown bear uses its claws like fingers to dig up and open razor clams on a beach in Katmai National Park, Alaska.

BROWN BEAR HABITS

Mother brown bears travel with their cubs. Adult males travel alone. Female bears fear the males because males sometimes attack and kill cubs.

Young bears that are no longer cubs, but not quite adults, often travel together in groups of two or three. The only time brown bears crowd together is at salmon streams.

Brown bears dig dens on hillsides in autumn. There they enter a deep sleep called **hibernation** (hi ber NAY shun).

Two brown bears fight over the rights to a fishing hole on an Alaska river.

BROWN BEAR COUSINS

The coastal brown bears' closest cousins are the brown bears that live inland, away from the sea. These bears, the grizzlies, are almost the same as coastal brown bears. They have the shoulder hump that all brown bears have. They are smaller than brownies, though. An average male grizzly in the southwestern Yukon Territory, for example, weighs just 306 pounds (139 kg)!

Just a few days before it enters hibernation, a grizzly looks for a berry patch on a hillside in central Alaska.

PEOPLE AND BEARS

People haven't always mixed well with brown bears. Bears of any kind can be dangerous. People fear brown bears the most. In the lower 48 states, grizzlies have almost been wiped out.

Alaska is different. It is rugged and wild, with few roads. Brown bears are plentiful.

More and more people are learning to respect and admire brown bears. Hundreds of people visit Alaska just to watch the great bears catch salmon.

This wild brown bear and the wildlife scientist seem to enjoy the McNeil River view—and each other's company.

SAVING ALASKA BROWN BEARS

There may be as many brown bears in Alaska now as there ever were. Alaska allows hunting of brownies, but hunting is carefully controlled.

The state provides a safe place for brown bears—and brown bear watchers—at the McNeil River Game **Sanctuary** (SANKT yu air ee). Hunting is not allowed in the sanctuary.

The U.S. Government also watches over bears on its land in Alaska. Katmai, Admiralty Island, Lake Clark National Parks, and Kodiak Island National Wildlife Refuge are homes for thousands of brownies.

Glossary

carnivore (KAR nih vor) — a meat-eating animal

graze (GRAYZ) — to feed by eating grass and other grasslike plants

hibernation (hi ber NAY shun) — the deep sleep some animals enter to survive the winter

salmon (SAH mun) — troutlike fish that are born in freshwater, grow up in the ocean, and return to freshwater to lay eggs

sanctuary (SANKT yu air ee) — an area set aside for the protection of plants and animals

INDEX